D1232036

# ALABAMA
## CRIMSON TIDE

BY K.C. KELLEY

Published by The Child's World®
1980 Lookout Drive • Mankato, MN 56003-1705
800-599-READ • www.childsworld.com

Cover: Vasha Hunt/AP Images.
Interior: AP Images: 11 ; Dreamstime.com: Suzye
4, 12; Newscom: Cliff Welch/Icon Sportswire 8;
Randy Litzinger/Icon 16; Jon Soohoo/UPI 19;
Michael Wade/Icon Sportwire 20; Shutterstock:
Jamie Lamor Thompson 15; Wikimedia: 7 (2).

ISBN 9781503850316 (Reinforced Library Binding)
ISBN 9781503850552 (Portable Document Format)
ISBN 9781503851313 (Online Multi-user eBook)
LCCN: 2021930283

Printed in the United States of America

*Great offense has helped Alabama win six national championships since 2009.*

# CONTENTS

# WHY WE LOVE COLLEGE FOOTBALL

The leaves are changing color. Happy crowds fill the stadiums. Pennants wave. And here come the fight songs! It's time for college football. The sport is one of America's most popular. Millions of fans follow their favorite teams. They wear school colors and hope for big wins.

*Alabama fans pack the stadium for every home game.*

One of the best football schools ever is the University of Alabama. The school has a long tradition of winning. Roll Tide!

# CHAPTER ONE

# Early Days

Alabama played its first football game in 1892. It won its first game 56-0. That kicked off a long and successful history.

In 1925, the school won its first national title. It had a 10-0 record. That season ended with a thrilling Rose Bowl game. The Crimson Tide beat Washington 20-19. Alabama won every game but one from 1925 through 1927.

The Southeastern **Conference** (SEC) began in 1933. That year, Alabama won the first of its 27 SEC titles.

## WHY CRIMSON TIDE?

Alabama's team nickname probably comes from its uniform colors. In the 1920s, sportswriters noted that the team "washed over" opponents!

University of Alabama
- Season 1920 -

*Above: The 1920 Alabama team showed off its striped-sleeve jerseys.*

*Left: The first Alabama team posed in 1892.*

# CHAPTER TWO

# Glory Years

In 1958, Paul "Bear" Bryant became Alabama's head coach. He led the school to six national titles. Bryant's first great season was in 1961. The Tide defense allowed only 25 points. Alabama went 11-0.

Bryant's team won back-to-back national titles in 1978 and 1979. The first came after a win in the Sugar Bowl. Alabama stopped Penn State at the **goal line** for a 14-7 win.

In 2007, Nick Saban took over as coach. He put Alabama back on top of college football. The school won six national titles between 2009 and 2020. Saban passed Bryant for most national championships. He now has seven, including six with 'Bama.

◄ *Bear Bryant was the Crimson Tide coach from 1958 to 1982. He was also a player for the team in the 1930s before becoming a coach.*

CHAPTER THREE

# Best Year Ever!

The 1979 team might have been Alabama's best. On defense, they gave up only 5.6 points per game. Only two **opponents** got more than 10 points. Alabama also had five **shutouts**. The offense piled up 31.9 points per game.

The Tide wrapped up a 12–0 season with a win in the Sugar Bowl. Running back Major Ogilvie scored twice. A 24–9 win made Alabama the national champs!

**ALABAMA'S PERFECT SEASONS**

| 1925 | 1934 | 1945 |
| 1961 | 1966 | 1979 |
| 1992 | 2009 | 2020 |

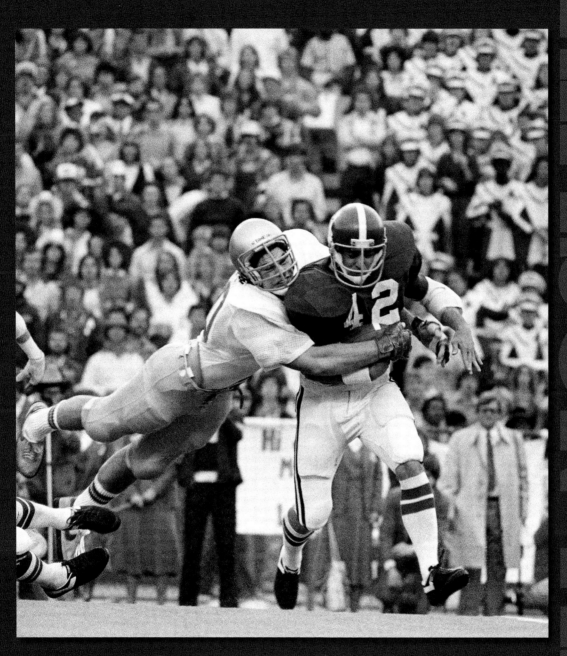

*Tough running like this helped Major Ogilvie (42)
lead the Crimson Tide in 1979.*

CHAPTER FOUR

# Alabama Traditions

Alabama football traditions have lasted for decades. Here are just a few of them:

• Fans sing "Rammer Jammer Yellow Hammer" whenever Alabama wins.

• Other favorite fan songs include "Sweet Home Alabama" and "Yea, Alabama."

• The most famous Alabama cheer is "Roll Tide Roll!"

## THE BIG RIVAL!

Alabama's biggest **rival** is Auburn. Auburn is also in the state of Alabama. The two schools have met every year since 1948. Their game is called the "Iron Bowl."

• Before home games, players and coaches take the Walk of Champions. They march to the stadium through a crowd of cheering students.

*"The Million Dollar Band" plays at every Alabama game. They sit together in Bryant-Denny Stadium.*

# CHAPTER FIVE

# Meet the Mascot

It would be hard to dress up as a Crimson Tide. So the Alabama **mascot** is an elephant. Why an elephant?

In 1930, a fan watched Alabama rumble onto the field. Some of the players were very large. The fan shouted, "The elephants are coming!" The 1930 team was named national champions. So the nickname stuck.

**HOME FIELD**

Bryant-Denny Stadium is named for the famous coach and a former school president. It was built in 1929 for 12,000 fans. It has grown a lot. Today, more than 101,000 Alabama **rooters** can pack inside.

In 1980, a student dressed in an elephant costume. Today, "Big Al" appears at all Alabama sporting events.

*Big Al has a female elephant mascot partner named Big Alice!* ➤

CHAPTER SIX

# Top Alabama QBs

Great teams need great quarterbacks (QBs). Alabama has had more than its share.

In the early 1940s, Harry Gilmer was an all-around star. He was the school's all-time leader in passing and running.

Joe Namath led the Tide to a national title in 1964. In the NFL, he became "Broadway Joe." He guided the New York Jets to Super Bowl III. They won! It was the biggest **upset** in NFL history.

Ken "The Snake" Stabler played from 1964 to 1967. He lost only two games as the **starting** QB.

A.J. McCarron was 36–4 at Alabama. He led the team to two national championships. In 2013, he won the Maxwell Award as the nation's best player.

*◄ A.J. McCarron led the Crimson Tide for three seasons.*
*He threw a total of 77 TD passes.*

# Other Alabama Heroes

Don Hutson was Alabama's first big superstar. His best years were 1934 and 1935. Hutson helped show that football teams should throw more passes. His speed and sure hands showed how important a receiver could be.

**Linebacker** Lee Roy Jordan was a defensive leader. In 1961, he was named to the **All-America** team. 'Bama won the national title.

Another linebacker was a star in the 1980s. Derrick Thomas piled up 52 **sacks** in three seasons. That's twice as many as any other Tide player. He won the 1988 Butkus Award as the top LB in the nation.

The Heisman Trophy is given to the best college player each year. Alabama won its first Heisman in 2009. Mark Ingram won after running for 1,648 yards.

*Mark Ingram leaps over the goal line for another touchdown.*
*His powerful running helped him win the Heisman Trophy.* ➤

# CHAPTER EIGHT

# Recent Superstars

In 2015, Derrick Henry earned Alabama's second Heisman Trophy. He ran for an SEC-record 2,219 yards. His 28 touchdowns helped the Tide win the national championship.

Minkah Fitzpatrick won the 2017 Bednarik Award. That goes to the top defensive player in the country.

QB Tua Tagovailoa came off the bench in the 2017 College Football Championship. Late in the game, he threw a game-winning TD! In 2018, he threw 43 TD passes. Now he is a star for the Miami Dolphins in the NFL.

In 2020, Devonta Smith became the first receiver to win the Heisman Trophy since 1991. He caught 20 TD passes. Smith had three TD catches in the national championship game. Alabama beat Ohio State 52–24.

◄ *Devonta Smith's speed and sure hands helped Alabama win the 2020 national championship over Ohio State.*

# GLOSSARY

**All-America** (ALL uh-MAYR-ih-kuh) an honor given to the top players in college sports

**conference** (KON-fur-enss) a group of schools that play sports against each other

**goal line** (GOHL LYNE) the white stripe at each end of the field past which teams have to move the ball to score a touchdown

**linebacker** (LYNE-bak-er) a defensive position that starts behind the defensive line

**mascot** (MASS-kot) a costumed character that leads cheers

**opponents** (uh-POH-nents) teams on the opposite side

**rival** (RYE-vul) a team faced often over a long period of time

**sacks** (SAX) tackles of the quarterback behind the line of scrimmage (where each play starts)

**shutouts** (SHUT-owts) games in which a team does not give up any points

**starting** (START-ing) the players who begin a game in the lineup

**upset** (UP-set) a win in a game a team was expected to lose

# FIND OUT MORE

## IN THE LIBRARY

Holmes, Parker. *Alabama vs. Auburn: College Football's Greatest Rivalries.* New York, NY: PowerKids Press, 2013.

Jacobs, Greg. *The Everything Kids' Football Book.* Avon, MA: Adams Media, 2018.

Meier, William. *Alabama Crimson Tide.* Minneapolis, MN: Lerner, 2020.

Weber, Margaret. *Alabama Crimson Tide.* Toronto, ON: Weigl, 2020.

## ON THE WEB

Visit our website for links about the
**Alabama Crimson Tide**:
**childsworld.com/links**

Note to Parents, Teachers, and Librarians: We routinely verify our Web links to make sure they are safe and active sites. So encourage your readers to check them out!

# INDEX

# ABOUT THE AUTHOR

**K.C. Kelley** is the author of more than 100 sports books for young readers, including numerous biographies of famous athletes. He went to the University of California—Berkeley, but his Golden Bears didn't quite make it into this series!